She glanced quickly at her mother, through wet lashes, and whimpered, "I don't know why they have to be so mean, is all."

Her mother kindly prompted, "Who was mean to you sweetie?"

"Never mind," Annie shook her head.

Bully-Be-Gone with Annie

By Michelle Fattig
Pictures by Josh Fattig

Experience Attention Deficits
Through the Eyes of a Child

Annie Books© Series
www.anniebooks.com

Flower by the Water Publishing Genoa, NE

iv

Annie Books © 2007

A Windy Day with Annie

A Prairie Day with Annie

Bully-Be-Gone with Annie

Viva Le Resistance!

Calming the Stormy Days with Annie

Coming soon to Annie Books:

Making Friends and Keeping Them with Annie

Learning to be Nice with Annie

Stopping the Blurting Days with Annie

Managing the Distracto-Days with Annie

This book is dedicated
to my wonderful husband,
amazing children, and
our family.

Text copyright © 2007 by Michelle Fattig.

Illustrations copyright © 2007 by Josh Fattig.

All rights reserved under international and Pan American Copyright Conventions. Published in the United States by Flower by the Water Publishing.

Fattig, Michelle. Bully-Be-Gone with Annie / Michelle Fattig ; Illustrated by Josh Fattig.

SUMMARY: In her own words, a young girl describes her feelings and emotions about bullies and the Bully-Be-Gone plan.

ISBN 978-0-9795805-5-0 (pbk)

ISBN 978-0-9795805-2-9 (ebk)

Manufactured in the United States of America.

Michelle and Josh
have Asperger's Syndrome and
Attention Deficit Disorder.
They use their unique insight and
experience to fight crime, battle
evil, and promote world peace.

"Annie! Time for breakfast!"

her mother called.

Annie snuggled more firmly

into her pillow.

"Annie, it's time to get up

and get ready for school."

Annie tearfully moaned,

"Mommy, my tummy hurts."

I don't think that I can go to school today."

Placing a hand on Annie's forehead, her mother asked, "Did you sleep okay?"

"Yes," Annie pitifully replied.

With her hand still on Annie's forehead, her mother

inquired, "Does your head hurt too?"

With a shuddering sigh, Annie answered, "Yes."

"Hmmm," her mother

responded with concern, "You

don't feel like you have a fever."

"My tummy really hurts though," Annie said, turning over and hugging her pillow tightly to her chest.

"Why don't you eat your breakfast and then we'll see how you feel, okay sweetie?"

"Mom?" Annie turned back towards her mother, as she was walking out of her room.

"Hmmm?"

"Can you drive me to school

from now on?" Annie asked with

a hopeful expression, and then quickly glanced downward.

Stopping and turning back towards Annie, her mother tilted her head slightly, and with a quizzical expression said, "What's wrong with the bus driver taking you to school?"

"I just like it when you drive me, that's all," Annie worried the edge of her pillow nervously between her fingers, "Mom, do you think I have a fat head?"

"What?" Annie's mom cried out.

She walked back over to the edge of Annie's bed and sat gingerly on the edge.

"Do you think that I have a fat head?" Annie repeated in a strained voice, nearly choking back a sob, but not completely

successful in her attempts.

Placing a hand gently on

Annie's arm, her mother replied,

"What do you mean; do you have

a fat head?"

Pulling away and tucking her

chin firmly down, Annie

shrugged, "Oh, it's nothing."

Her mother watched Annie for a few seconds, and then stood, suggesting, "Why don't you get up and get dressed now?"

"Mom," Annie whined, "my tummy still really hurts."

Her mother looked on

thoughtfully for a few more

seconds, and then sat back down

next to Annie.

Using two fingers, she gently

tipped Annie's face up towards

her own and asked softly, "Did

something happen on the bus that

you want to talk to me about?"

Sniffing, Annie dropped her

head back, as if working her

bedding nervously between her

fingers was the most interesting of tasks.

She glanced quickly up at her mother, through wet lashes, and whimpered, "I don't know why they have to be so mean, is all."

Her mother kindly prompted, "Who was mean to you sweetie?"

"Never mind," Annie shook her head.

Not ready to give the subject up, her mom pulled Annie into her arms and squeezed, "No, come here for a minute please. Who was mean to you? Who said that you have a fat head?"

Taking a deep breath, still trying to keep the tears at bay, Annie said quietly, "It's just some kids. They say mean things sometimes."

"Do they say mean things to everyone?"

"No, pretty much just me."

"When they say things to
you, how does it make you feel?"

sniff

"I don't want to talk about it right now, my tummy really hurts."

"You feel sad when they say mean things," her mother prompted.

sniff

She continued, "Do the kids ever hit you?"

"No. But, sniff they say, 'Fat head, fat head, go away and don't come out some other day.'"

After a few moments pause, her mother prompted again, "That doesn't sound very nice at all."

"I just don't want to ride the bus anymore mom, please."

Annie threw herself back into her pillow, face first, and sobbed.

"What do you think would happen if you stopped riding the bus?"

"They couldn't say mean things to me anymore," came the muffled reply.

Stroking Annie's hair, her mother asked, "Don't you see them in the hallways?"

"Yes."

"Don't you see them at lunch?"

"Yes."

"Don't you have any classes with them?"

"Yes."

Her mother gently tugged

Annie back into her arms and said

softly, "Don't you see that not

riding the bus isn't going to solve

the problem?"

sniff

"Could we just move away?"

Sighing, Annie's mother

replied, "Well sweetie, as much as

I'd like to move you away from

any pain, it just wouldn't work.

You see, there are going to be

mean spirited people wherever you go. Sometimes it is good to figure out why someone is mean and to learn how to cope with it, rather than running away."

"But I'd rather just move away! Then they can't laugh and call me a fat head anymore," Annie wailed.

"Why do you think kids say
mean things?"

"Because I'm fat and ugly
and stupid and nobody likes me."

With a wrinkled forehead,

Annie's mother said firmly,

"That's not true. You are sweet,

kind, smart, funny, and very, very

cute."

sniff

"Maybe if you like fat

heads!"

"Do you think that you have

a fat head?"

"Maybe."

"Look at me please," more firmly, her mother continued, "Do you *really* think that you have a fat head?"

After a brief pause, Annie looked up, "No. At least I never thought that before. It's just that sometimes it makes me feel like I don't have any friends when they

say mean things to me. Nobody

even sticks up for me Mom!"

"Do you know what a bully
is?" Annie's mother asked,
looking off into nowhere in
particular. In Annie's family that
look was known as the 'thousand-
yard-stare.'

"Yes," Annie shook her head
and wiped her nose with the back
of her hand, "Mr. Caton, the

counselor, talks about bullying in

homeroom sometimes."

"Do you know that the kids

who are saying mean things, are

usually very sad and hurt?"

Annie looked confused,

"What do you mean?"

"Sometimes kids become
bullies, when they see things in
others, that are most like
themselves.

Sometimes kids become
bullies, because their mommy or
daddy isn't very nice to them at
home, or their brothers and sisters
pick on them, so they feel the need
to hurt somebody else, to cover up
their own hurt feelings.

Sometimes, kids pick out
kids to bully, who seem sad,

alone, or different. They pick on

them, so they don't feel like the

one being picked on.

Sometimes kids become

bullies, because their mommy and

daddy are getting a divorce or they

don't have enough money for

bills.

Sometimes the kids who bully, don't actually realize how hurtful their words can be.

Sometimes kids become bullies, because that's the way they are treated at home, and they think it is normal.

Sometimes kids become bullies, because they want to seem

cool to other students, or to try and

fit in, because they feel left out.

The most important thing to know

about bullies is that they are not

the most important people in your

life."

"It feels that way

sometimes," Annie gloomily

replied.

"I know it does. It's hard to

understand, but bullies are just like

you or me, but with problems.

You don't need to be afraid, or to

43

fight back. Bullies should be

pitied, since they are obviously

very insecure or unhappy in their

life."

"But why do they have to call

me a fat head?"

"Because they feel mad or

sad about themselves, so they pick

on other people."

"But that's not fair!" Annie

shouted indignantly.

"I know it's not," her mother

responded, "Would you like to

figure out some ways to make

them stop bullying you?"

"Yeah right! How am I

going to do that?"

"Well, let's talk about a plan.

"A Bully-be-gone Plan!"

Annie and her mother shouted and

laughed together.

Annie's mother hugged her tightly and said, "The real key to getting them to stop, is to care about *you,* enough to stay calm. Bullies only want to upset you. They want to have control over you and your emotions. Each time you get upset, you are giving the bullies more power."

"But it's hard to stay calm!"

"I know sweetie. Let's think of some ways to stay calm. You could breathe deeply, in through your nose and out through your mouth, counting slowly to ten."

"Oh mom, you always tell me to do that when I get mad at my sister."

"Yes I do, and does it work?"

"Sometimes it does!"

"Good," Annie's mother said with a smile, "what else could you try to do that will help you stay calm?"

"I could write."

"Good, writing in a journal is a great way to stay calm and help to put things into perspective."

"Bully-be-gone stay CALM!"

Annie and her mother again

shouted together, this time, openly

laughing.

"Another thing you could try,

when they are bullying you or

calling names, is to look them

directly in the eye and say, "I want

you to stop," and walk away or

turn away. Keep your head up and

try to stay relaxed. That way you

aren't giving the bullies any more power. Ignoring can be the most effective way of stopping bullies in their tracks!"

"Why?"

"Because it is just no fun for the bully, if there isn't a victim anymore," her mother pointed out wisely, "Bully-be-gone Stop!

Keep your head up, stay relaxed,

and IGNORE!"

"What if walking away or

telling them to stop doesn't

work?"

"Sometimes, laughing with

the bullies, or saying something

like, "Good one," can throw off a

bully. But don't make fun of the

bully, since that is like fighting."

"Fighting doesn't work,"

Annie replied, nodding gravely.

"You are right. It is always

best to walk away from a fight, her

mother smiled approvingly with a

brief, but firm nod of her head.

"Bully-be-gone Laughter is the BEST Medicine!" You did the right thing by talking with me about the bullies. Telling an adult is very important whenever you feel sad, scared, hurt or afraid. There are lots of adults that you could tell at school. Can you think of anyone you could go to if you are being bullied?"

"I guess the principal or my teacher, but she says 'no tattling' or 'work it out yourselves.'"

"It's not tattling if you or your things are hurt by a bully. It's very important that you know that you can talk to someone about your feelings, if you feel like you

are being bullied. It is never okay

to hurt alone or in silence. You

never know, if you ignore the

bullies or tell an adult, more kids

might feel safe talking about the

bullies too. You are probably not

the only one who is feeling picked

on."

"Bully-be-gone TALK it OUT!" Annie and her mother repeated together, this time with a smile.

"I think my tummy feels a little better now."

"That's great honey! Do you think you are ready to get dressed for school?"

"I guess so."

"Do you think you are ready to ride the bus?"

"I guess so."

"Do you think you are ready to use your plan to take away the bullies' power?"

"Yes!" Annie stated firmly.

"That's great! I think you are ready too!"

We hope you have enjoyed Bully-Be-Gone with Annie. For more Annie Books see:
www.anniebooks.com

Michelle, Josh, and Lilianne

www.ingramcontent.com/pod-product-compliance
Lightning Source LLC
Chambersburg PA
CBHW050606280326
41933CB00011B/2002